This is the true story of Legadema, a little leopard who learned to go out on her own in a big, big world.

NATIONAL
GEOGRAPHIC
KiDS

A Leap for
Legadema

The True Story of a Little
Leopard in a Big World

Beverly and Dereck Joubert

NATIONAL GEOGRAPHIC
WASHINGTON, D.C.

Every leopard's spots are one of a kind. You will know *this* leopard by a unique round spot between the two top rows of whiskers, to the right of her nose.

Look for her spot as you read this story.

egadema (pronounced *LA-ga-dee-ma*) was born at the end of autumn and was given her name after a fantastic African storm, when the dark sky cracked and brightened with lightning. Legadema means "light from the sky" in the Setswana language.

Her home was an island in the heart of the Okavango Delta, in Botswana, Africa. Thick with animals, the Okavango is a noisy, chirping, squeaking, trumpeting, bellowing, roaring Eden. The musty scent of wet Kalahari sands, animals, wild sage, and acacia blossoms fills the air.

Legadema's mother, Tortilis, was a queen—the queen of the acacias. She loved to spend time in the acacia trees after which she was named, where she leaped through the canopy like a high-wire acrobat. She also loved to lie in the hollow of an ancient baobab, or drape herself along its branches to watch the world.

Tortilis had been a mother before, but Legadema was her first cub to survive.

The wild is a dangerous place for a leopard cub, so Legadema had to first learn how to hide while her mother went off to find food.

Legadema's mother taught her little leopard everything she needed to know to be independent and to survive in the big, big world.

She taught her how to climb a tree.

It's not as easy as it looks! Legadema's mother once had to grab her by the neck with her teeth to keep her from falling to the ground below.

She taught her how to watch for danger and to disappear instantly.

Legadema copied her mother's every step, but she knew when she'd been caught: A sudden flurry of birds—cisticolas, starlings, and shrikes—and the bark and chatter of squirrels, baboons, and monkeys would announce her presence.

Legadema's mother taught her how to stalk, hunt, and kill prey.

One day, when Legadema spotted a small creature thumping in the grass, she quietly stalked it and carried out the perfect hunt . . . of her mama's tail!

Mother and cub were such friends that they were often just a jumble of spots, tousling, biting, growling, licking, and cuddling up together. Each day that Legadema's mother was playing with her, she was teaching her how to be a big leopard.

When crimson clouds
blanketed the horizon
and the forest
came alive with a cacophony
of animals and an orchestra
of frogs that sounded like tiny
bells, Legadema's mother carried

her cub in her mouth and settled into their sheltered den. But even in sleep, a leopard never lets her guard down. Alert ears work the sounds of the forest.

When Legadema was three months old, her mother left her alone to go hunt.

Legadema knew how to entertain herself. She stalked hissing frogs and lizards. She chewed on a tortoise shell. She chased squirrels up and down and around the trees. Legadema *loved* chasing squirrels. But they are so hard to catch!

She bounded after butterflies, and she patted at furry pink cattail flowers.

Legadema always knew when her mother was close. They shared a secret call, a raspy grunt.

One day, Legadema was so busy that she didn't notice the lions nearby. Her mother, back from her hunt, didn't either—she was focused on Legadema, keeping track of her wandering cub. They were about to become the lions' lunch!

The lions roared and Legadema's mother bolted, making such a show of leaping up into a tree that it distracted the lions. The lions chased her mother, giving Legadema the chance to slip away into the thickets and stay hidden while her mother stared down the lions.

Fortunately, most lions can't climb trees. So her mother waited up high until the lions fell asleep beneath the tree, and then she leaped to safety.

Soon little Legadema was no longer little. It was time for her to explore the big world on her own. It was time for her to find her own home, apart from her mother, as every leopard must do.

At first, like any young adult, Legadema survived on a fast-food diet—squirrels! Now that Legadema was older and quicker, she could catch them. Lots of them.

Alone, she wandered the bush. Sometimes she hid in trees like she did as a cub and watched the evening sky turn from dim orange to scarlet to ink, but it wasn't quite home.

Some days, Legadema caught her mother's scent. Other days, Legadema heard her mother's secret call, and she knew she was close.

When they would meet, they'd greet each other with a quick look and part again. It was the lesson of life, and they both knew Legadema needed to be independent.

Eventually, Legadema found the perfect home in her own territory. She settled into a hollowed-out log the size of a small boat.

Legadema's mom had taught her well: Legadema was taking care of herself now. And just in time . . .

One day the following summer, when dawn broke in the heart of the Okavango Delta, in Botswana, Africa, a mother, named after a storm, woke to nurse two little cubs of her own—Pula, named after the rain, and Maru, which means "cloud."

Legadema was all grown up. Now it was her turn to teach her two cubs to leap.

Legadema's home
and where leopards live in Africa

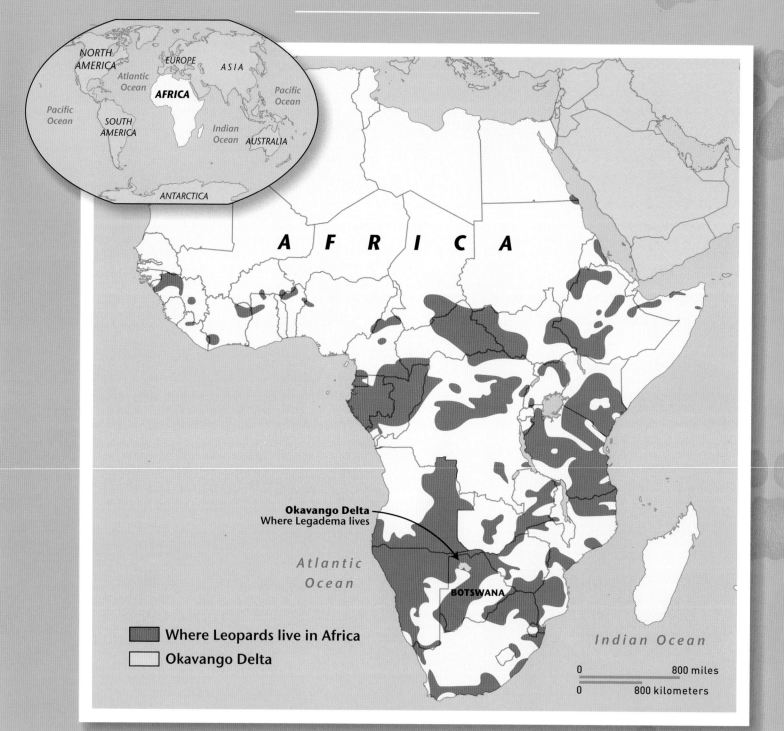

NORTH
AMERICA
EUROPE
ASIA
AFRICA
Atlantic
Ocean
Pacific
Ocean
Pacific
Ocean
SOUTH
AMERICA
Indian
Ocean
AUSTRALIA
ANTARCTICA

A F R I C A

Okavango Delta
Where Legadema lives

Atlantic
Ocean

BOTSWANA

Indian Ocean

Where Leopards live in Africa
Okavango Delta

0   800 miles
0   800 kilometers

Want to learn more about leopards?

ORGANIZATIONS & WEBSITES

National Geographic's Big Cats Initiative
nationalgeographic.org/projects/big-cats-initiative

National Geographic
animals.nationalgeographic.com/animals/mammals/leopard

BOOKS & VIDEOS

Eye of the Leopard (book), by Dereck and Beverly Joubert. Rizzoli, 2009.

Eye of the Leopard (DVD), by Dereck and Beverly Joubert. National Geographic, 2007.

Eye of the Leopard (app), by Dereck and Beverly Joubert. Available on iTunes for iPad. itunes.apple.com/us/app/eye-of-the-leopard/id1065755145?mt=8

Face to Face With Leopards (book), by Dereck and Beverly Joubert. National Geographic, 2009.

PLACES TO SEE LEOPARDS

Great Plains Conservation
greatplainsconservation.com

About Legadema and Leopards

- Most leopards are beige colored and have dark spots on their fur. These spots are called rosettes because their shape is similar to that of a rose.

- Leopards live in sub-Saharan Africa, northeast Africa, Central Asia, India, and China.

- Leopards are fast! They can run at up to 36 miles an hour (60 km/h), but just for short bursts. They're super springy, too, and can leap six yards (5.5 m) forward through the air—that's the length of three adults lying head to toe.

- Leopards are solitary and spend most of their time alone. They each have their own territory, and they leave scratches on trees, urine scent marks, and poop to warn other leopards to stay away!

- Leopards eat fish, antelope, monkeys, rodents—pretty much any prey that is available.

- Leopards can climb trees, and they like to rest on tree branches during the day. They are strong, too; they carry their heavy prey up into the trees so that pesky scavengers, like hyenas, don't steal their meal!

- Leopards are often nocturnal, which means they are active at night when they venture out in search of food, but they do hunt during the day in places they are safe. They spend their days mostly resting, camouflaged in the trees or hiding in thickets.

- Female leopards usually give birth to two or three cubs at a time. Mothers stay with their cubs until they are about 18 months old (when they are old enough to hunt and take care of themselves).

- Leopards communicate with each other through distinctive calls such as a raspy, sawing sound. They also hiss and growl when angry, and make slight contact calls that sound like gentle coughs.

A note from the photographers

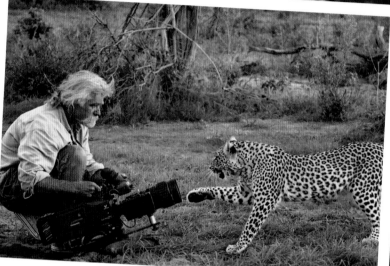

We spent four and half years living with Legadema. It changed our lives. Because her mom was often away, we were kind of like babysitters, just watching a sleeping cub most of the first three months. Then she started recognizing us, individually, and would come up every few hours and greet us, often by looking up into Beverly's eyes and then sometimes gently biting my foot in greeting, never aggressively. And even though we never touched her, she touched our hearts and turned us from being just filmmakers and explorers or conservationists into advocates for leopards. We started the National Geographic Big Cats Initiative as a result, and now we are active in saving big cats just like Legadema in more than 27 countries.

We can all make a difference and save big cats like Legadema.

—Beverly and Dereck Joubert

As filmmakers and photographers in the wild, the Jouberts always do their best to blend into the environment and to not interfere with nature. But sometimes their subjects spot them and are more than a little curious! Here, Legadema gives Dereck's camera a playful pat.

Credits

This book is dedicated to Legadema, and the protection of all leopards in Africa.
—Beverly and Dereck Joubert

Since 1888, the National Geographic Society has funded more than 12,000 research, exploration, and preservation projects around the world. The Society receives funds from National Geographic Partners, LLC, funded in part by your purchase. A portion of the proceeds from this book supports this vital work. To learn more, visit natgeo.com/info.

NATIONAL GEOGRAPHIC and Yellow Border Design are trademarks of the National Geographic Society, used under license.

For more information, visit nationalgeographic.com, call 1-800-647-5463, or write to the following address:

National Geographic Partners
1145 17th Street N.W.
Washington, D.C. 20036-4688 U.S.A.

Visit us online at nationalgeographic.com/books

For librarians and teachers: ngchildrensbooks.org

More for kids from National Geographic: kids.nationalgeographic.com

For information about special discounts for bulk purchases, please contact National Geographic Books Special Sales: specialsales@natgeo.com

For rights or permissions inquiries, please contact National Geographic Books Subsidiary Rights: bookrights@natgeo.com

The publisher would like to thank everyone who helped make this book possible: Amy Novesky, contributing writer; Ariane Szu-Tu, associate editor; Sarah J. Mock, senior photo editor; Alix Inchausti, production editor; and Anne LeongSon and Gus Tello, design production assistants.

Designed by Callie Broaddus

Hardcover ISBN: 978-1-4263-2973-9
Reinforced library binding ISBN: 978-1-4263-2974-6

Printed in Hong Kong
17/THK/1

Page 31, Corly and Arjen Vons. All other photos copyright © Beverly Joubert.

A NOTE ON THE DESIGN

Legadema was born in the Okavango Delta, in Botswana, Africa, a land defined by its abundant life. The illustrations used throughout the design of this book are inspired by the landscape of Legadema's home. The lala palm tree, or fan palm, with its long, slender trunks and round, clustered fruits, provided inspiration for the border pattern scattered through these pages. The color palette was chosen to reflect the dry grasses and lush forests, and illustrations of lala palm trees, elephant grass, and leopard tracks help keep young readers engaged on every page.

Left: Lala palm trees (*Hyphaene petersiana*)

Right: A leopard print in the sand